A Dragon in a Wagon

by Jane Belk Moncure
illustrated by Linda Hohag

Published by THE CHILD'S WORLD®

Mankato, Minnesota

GROLIER BOOKS

Grolier Books is a division of
Grolier Enterprises, Inc.,
Danbury, CT.

The Library — A Magic Castle

Come to the magic castle
When you are growing tall.
Rows upon rows of Word Windows
Line every single wall.
They reach up high,
As high as the sky,
And you want to open them all.
For every time you open one,
A new adventure has begun.

Megan opens a Word Window.
Guess what she sees?

A dragon
in a wagon.

"Hi," says the dragon. "Let's
go for a ride."

"Good idea," says Megan.

She hops inside.

But the wagon does not go very far, so . . .

Megan and the dragon hop into a car.
The car will not go, so they . . .

hop on a bus . . .

with a horse and a fat hippopotamus.

The bus will not go, so they . . .

jump into a boat . . .

with a dog, three cats, and a billy goat.

The boat will not float, so they . . .

hop on a sled . . .

with a moose who has five funny mice
on his head.

The sled will not go, so they . . .

jump on
a truck
with . . .

a cow, three pigs, a hen, and a duck.

The truck will not go, so they . . .

hop on a train . . .

with an elephant and a
long-legged crane.

The train will not go. And it starts to . . .

rain, so they hop off the train
and step into a plane.

The plane will not fly, so they . . .

float in
the sky.

"Where are you going?" asks a bird,
flying by.

"I don't know," says Megan.
"But we'll be there soon."

As soon as
they land,

they find a balloon.

"Whee," says the dragon.

"Let's fly to the moon.

Let's keep on going . . . and fly to a star."

"Oh no,"
says Megan.

"I will not go that far. I think we should
stop. Do you see where we are?"

Megan waves to a clown and
a girl on a swing. But then . . .

the dragon finds his favorite thing.
"Come along," says the dragon
as he rides away.

"No, thank you," says Megan. "No
more rides today. Good-bye, dragon
in a wagon."

You can read these words with Megan.

wagon

sled

boat

bus

car

truck